POETICS

DOVER THRIFT EDITIONS

Aristotle

DOVER PUBLICATIONS
GARDEN CITY, NEW YORK

DOVER THRIFT EDITIONS
GENERAL EDITOR: STANLEY APPELBAUM
EDITOR OF THIS VOLUME: RICHARD KOSS

Copyright

Bibliographical Note

This Dover edition, first published in 1997, is an unabridged republication of S. H. Butcher's translation of the *Poetics* as originally published by Macmillan and Co., London, as part of the volume *Aristotle's Theory of Poetry and Fine Art* in 1895. A new Note, and footnotes translating the Greek quotations, have been added to this edition.

Library of Congress Cataloging-in-Publication Data

Aristotle
    [Poetics. English]
    Poetics/Aristotle.
       p. cm. — (Dover thrift editions.)
    "Unabridged republication of S.H. Butcher's translation of the Poetics as originally published by Macmillan and Co., London, as part of the volume Aristotle's theory of poetry and fine arts in 1895 [with] a new Note, and footnotes translating the Greek quotations" — T.p. verso.
    ISBN-13: 978-0-486-29577-0 (pbk.)
    ISBN-10: 0-486-29577-X (pbk.)
    1. Poetry—Early works to 1800. 2. Aesthetics—Early works to 1800. I. Butcher, S. H. (Samuel Henry), 1850–1910. II. Title. III. Series.
PN1040.A513   1997
808.2—dc21
                                    96-47116
                                    CIP

Manufactured in the United States of America
29577X18   2023
www.doverpublications.com

Note

ARGUABLY THE MOST SIGNIFICANT critical work of antiquity, Aristotle's *Poetics* represents the first major analysis of Hellenic literature as well as the first attempt to distinguish between literary genres. Written circa 330 B.C., it is a reservoir of the themes and schemes deployed in ancient Greek tragedy and epic poetry (a further volume, believed to have been devoted to comedy, has not survived). The *Poetics*, moreover, presents a fine glimpse of Aristotelian thought.

Born in 384 in Stagira near Macedonia, Aristotle moved at the age of 17 to Athens where he spent the subsequent 20 years as the most brilliant student in Plato's Academy. Although in his *Republic* Plato condemned the arts as an imitator of things that were themselves imitations of ultimate reality, Aristotle was to verge from his mentor in the *Poetics*, recognizing the light both tragic drama and epic poetry shed on the human condition. Following Plato's death in 347, Aristotle left Athens to travel, settling in 343 in Macedonia where he served as the tutor to the young Alexander the Great. In 335, he returned to Athens where he founded his own school, the Lyceum, which was to continue for several centuries after his death in 322.

Though much of his work has not survived him, the influence of Aristotle on Western philosophy is immense. The *Poetics* transcends the age in which it was written as well as the ancient art forms it investigated, setting, as T. S. Eliot observed, "an eternal example . . . of intelligence itself swiftly operating the analysis of sensation to the point of principle and definition."

I

I PROPOSE to treat of Poetry in itself and of its various kinds, noting the essential quality of each; to inquire into the structure of the plot as requisite to a good poem; into the number and nature of the parts of which a poem is composed; and similarly into whatever else falls within the same inquiry. Following, then, the order of nature, let us begin with the principles which come first.

Epic poetry and Tragedy, Comedy also and Dithyrambic poetry, and the music of the flute and of the lyre in most of their forms, are all in their general conception modes of imitation. They differ, however, from one another in three respects, — the medium, the objects, the manner or mode of imitation, being in each case distinct.

For as there are persons who, by conscious art or mere habit, imitate and represent various objects through the medium of colour and form, or again by the voice; so in the arts above mentioned, taken as a whole, the imitation is produced by rhythm, language, or 'harmony,' either singly or combined.

Thus in the music of the flute and of the lyre, 'harmony' and rhythm alone are employed; also in other arts, such as that of the shepherd's pipe, which are essentially similar to these. In dancing, rhythm alone is used without 'harmony'; for even dancing imitates character, emotion, and action, by rhythmical movement.

There is another art which imitates by means of language alone, and that either in prose or verse — which verse, again, may either combine different metres or consist of but one kind — but this has hitherto been without a name. For there is no common term we could apply to the mimes of Sophron and Xenarchus and the Socratic dialogues on the one hand; and, on the other, to poetic imitations in iambic, elegiac, or any similar metre. People do, indeed, add the word 'maker' or 'poet' to the name of the metre, and speak of elegiac poets, or epic (that is, hexameter) poets, as if it were not the imitation that makes the poet, but the verse that entitles them all indiscriminately to the name. Even when a treatise on medicine or natural science is brought out in verse, the name of poet is by custom given to the author; and yet Homer and Empedocles have nothing in common but the metre, so that it would be right to call the one poet, the other physicist rather than poet. On the same principle, even if a writer in his poetic imitation were to combine all metres, as Chaeremon did in his Centaur, which is a medley composed of metres of all kinds, we should bring him too under the general term poet. So much then for these distinctions.

There are, again, some arts which employ all the means above mentioned, — namely, rhythm, tune, and metre. Such are Dithyrambic and Nomic poetry, and also Tragedy and Comedy; but between them the difference is, that in the first two cases these means are all employed in combination, in the latter, now one means is employed, now another.

Such, then, are the differences of the arts with respect to the medium of imitation.

II

Since the objects of imitation are men in action, and these men must be either of a higher or a lower type (for moral character mainly answers to these divisions, goodness and badness being the distinguishing marks of moral differences), it follows that we must represent men either as better than in real life, or as worse, or as they are. It is the same in painting. Polygnotus depicted men as nobler than they are, Pauson as less noble, Dionysius drew them true to life.

Now it is evident that each of the modes of imitation above mentioned will exhibit these differences, and become a distinct kind in imitating objects that are thus distinct. Such diversities may be found even in dancing, flute-playing, and lyre-playing. So again in language, whether prose or verse unaccompanied by music. Homer, for example, makes men better than they are; Cleophon as they are; Hegemon the Thasian, the inventor of parodies, and Nicochares, the author of the Deiliad, worse than they are. The same thing holds good of Dithyrambs and Nomes; here too one may portray different types, as Timotheus and Philoxenus differed in representing their Cyclopes. The same distinction marks off Tragedy from Comedy; for Comedy aims at representing men as worse, Tragedy as better than in actual life.

III

There is still a third difference — the manner in which each of these objects may be imitated. For the medium being the same, and the objects the same, the poet may imitate by narration — in which case he can either take another personality as Homer does, or speak in his own person, unchanged — or he may present all his characters as living and moving before us.

These, then, as we said at the beginning, are the three differences which distinguish artistic imitation, — the medium, the objects, and the manner. So that from one point of view, Sophocles is an imitator of the same kind as Homer — for both imitate higher types of character; from another point of view, of the same kind as Aristophanes — for both imitate persons acting and doing. Hence, some say, the name of 'drama' is given to such poems, as representing action. For the same reason the Dorians claim the invention both of Tragedy and Comedy. The claim to Comedy is put forward by the Megarians, — not only by those of Greece proper, who allege that it originated under their democracy, but also by the Megarians of Sicily, for the poet Epicharmus, who is much earlier than Chionides and Magnes, belonged to that country. Tragedy too is claimed by certain Dorians of the Peloponnese. In each case they appeal to the evidence of language. The outlying villages, they say, are by them called κῶμαι, by the Athenians δῆμοι: and they assume that Comedians were so named not from κωμάζειν, 'to revel,' but because they wandered from village to village (κατὰ κώμας), being excluded contemptuously from the city. They add also that the Dorian word for 'doing' is δρᾶν, and the Athenian, πράττειν.

This may suffice as to the number and nature of the various modes of imitation.

IV

Poetry in general seems to have sprung from two causes, each of them lying deep in our nature. First, the instinct of imitation is implanted in man from childhood, one difference between him and other animals being that he is the most imitative of living creatures, and through imitation learns his earliest lessons; and no less universal is the pleasure felt in things imitated. We have evidence of this in the facts of experience. Objects which in themselves we view with pain, we delight to contemplate when reproduced with minute fidelity: such as the forms of the most ignoble animals and of dead bodies. The cause of this again is, that to learn gives the liveliest pleasure, not only to philosophers but to men in general; whose capacity, however, of learning is more limited. Thus the reason why men enjoy seeing a likeness is, that in contemplating it they find themselves learning or inferring, and saying perhaps, 'Ah, that is he.' For if you happen not to have seen the original, the pleasure will be due not to the imitation as such, but to the execution, the colouring, or some such other cause.

Imitation, then, is one instinct of our nature. Next, there is the instinct for 'harmony' and rhythm, metres being manifestly sections of rhythm. Persons, therefore, starting with this natural gift developed by degrees their special aptitudes, till their rude improvisations gave birth to Poetry.

Poetry now diverged in two directions, according to the individual character of the writers. The graver spirits imitated noble actions, and the actions of good men. The more trivial sort imitated the actions of meaner persons, at first composing satires, as the former did hymns to the gods and the praises of famous men. A poem of the satirical kind cannot indeed be put down to any author earlier than Homer; though many such writers probably there were. But from Homer onward, instances can be cited, — his own Margites, for example, and other similar compositions. The appropriate metre was also here introduced; hence the measure is still called the iambic or lampooning measure, being that in which people lampooned one another. Thus the older poets were distinguished as writers of heroic or of lampooning verse.

As, in the serious style, Homer is pre-eminent among poets, for he alone combined dramatic form with excellence of imitation, so he too first laid down the main lines of Comedy, by dramatising the ludicrous instead of writing personal satire. His Margites bears the same relation to Comedy that the Iliad and Odyssey do to Tragedy. But when Tragedy and Comedy came to light, the two classes of poets still followed their natural bent: the lampooners became writers of Comedy, and the Epic poets were succeeded by Tragedians, since the drama was a larger and higher form of art.

Whether Tragedy has as yet perfected its proper types or not; and whether it is to be judged in itself, or in relation also to the audience, — this raises another question. Be that as it may, Tragedy — as also Comedy — was at first mere improvisation. The one originated with the authors of the Dithyramb, the other with those of the phallic songs, which are still in use in many of our cities. Tragedy advanced by slow degrees; each new element that showed itself was in turn developed. Having passed through many changes, it found its natural form, and there it stopped.

Aeschylus first introduced a second actor; he diminished the importance of the Chorus, and assigned the leading part to the dialogue. Sophocles raised the number of actors to three, and added scene-painting. Moreover, it was not till late that the short plot was discarded for one of greater compass, and the grotesque diction of the earlier satyric form for the stately manner of Tragedy. The iambic measure then replaced the trochaic tetrameter, which was originally employed when the poetry was of the satyric order, and had greater affinities with dancing. Once dialogue had come in, Nature herself discovered the appropriate measure. For the iambic is, of all measures, the most colloquial: we see it in the fact that conversational speech runs into iambic lines more frequently than into any other kind of verse; rarely into hexameters, and only when we drop the colloquial intonation. The additions to the number of 'episodes' or acts, and the other accessories of which tradition tells, must be taken as already described; for to discuss them in detail would, doubtless, be a large undertaking.

V

Comedy is, as we have said, an imitation of characters of a lower type, — not, however, in the full sense of the word bad, the Ludicrous being merely a subdivision of the ugly. It consists in some defect or ugliness which is not painful or destructive. To take an obvious example, the comic mask is ugly and distorted, but does not imply pain.

The successive changes through which Tragedy passed, and the authors of these changes, are well known, whereas Comedy has had no history, because it was not at first treated seriously. It was late before the Archon granted a comic chorus to a poet; the performers were till then voluntary. Comedy had already taken definite shape when comic poets, distinctively so called, are heard of. Who furnished it with masks, or prologues, or increased the number of actors, — these and other similar details remain unknown. As for the plot, it came originally from Sicily; but of Athenian writers Crates was the first who, abandoning the 'iambic' or lampooning form, generalised his themes and plots.

Epic poetry agrees with Tragedy in so far as it is an imitation in verse of characters of a higher type. They differ, in that Epic poetry admits but one kind of metre, and is narrative in form. They differ, again, in their length: for Tragedy endeavours, as far as possible, to confine itself to a single revolution of the sun, or but slightly to exceed this limit; whereas the Epic action has no limits of time. This, then, is a second point of difference; though at first the same freedom was admitted in Tragedy as in Epic poetry.

Of their constituent parts some are common to both, some peculiar to Tragedy: whoever, therefore, knows what is good or bad Tragedy, knows also about Epic poetry. All the elements of an Epic poem are found in Tragedy, but the elements of a Tragedy are not all found in the Epic poem.

VI

Of the poetry which imitates in hexameter verse, and of Comedy, we will speak hereafter. Let us now discuss Tragedy, resuming its formal definition, as resulting from what has been already said.

Tragedy, then, is an imitation of an action that is serious, complete, and of a certain magnitude; in language embellished with each kind of artistic ornament, the several kinds being found in separate parts of the play; in the form of action, not of narrative; through pity and fear effecting the proper purgation of these emotions. By 'language embellished,' I mean language into which rhythm, 'harmony,' and song enter. By 'the several kinds in separate parts,' I mean, that some parts are rendered through the medium of verse alone, others again with the aid of song.

Now as tragic imitation implies persons acting, it necessarily follows, in the first place, that Spectacular equipment will be a part of Tragedy. Next, Song and Diction, for these are the medium of imitation. By 'Diction' I mean the mere metrical arrangement of the words: as for 'Song,' it is a term whose sense every one understands.

Again, Tragedy is the imitation of an action; and an action implies personal agents, who necessarily possess certain distinctive qualities both of character and thought; for it is by these that we qualify actions themselves, and these — thought and character — are the two natural causes from which actions spring, and on actions again all success or failure depends. Hence, the Plot is the imitation of the action: — for by plot I here mean the arrangement of the incidents. By Character I mean that in virtue of which we ascribe certain qualities to the agents. Thought is required wherever a statement is proved, or, it may be, a general truth enunciated. Every Tragedy, therefore, must have six parts, which parts determine its quality — namely, Plot, Character, Diction, Thought, Spectacle, Song. Two of the parts constitute the medium of imitation, one the manner, and three the objects of imitation. And these complete the list. These elements have been employed, we may say, by the poets to a man; in fact, every play contains Spectacular elements as well as Character, Plot, Diction, Song, and Thought.

But most important of all is the structure of the

incidents. For Tragedy is an imitation, not of men, but of an action and of life, and life consists in action, and its end is a mode of action, not a quality. Now character determines men's qualities, but it is by their actions that they are happy or the reverse. Dramatic action, therefore, is not with a view to the representation of character: character comes in as subsidiary to the actions. Hence the incidents and the plot are the end of a tragedy; and the end is the chief thing of all. Again, without action there cannot be a tragedy; there may be without character. The tragedies of most of our modern poets fail in the rendering of character; and of poets in general this is often true. It is the same in painting; and here lies the difference between Zeuxis and Polygnotus. Polygnotus delineates character well: the style of Zeuxis is devoid of ethical quality. Again, if you string together a set of speeches expressive of character, and well finished in point of diction and thought, you will not produce the essential tragic effect nearly so well as with a play which, however deficient in these respects, yet has a plot and artistically constructed incidents. Besides which, the most powerful elements of emotional interest in Tragedy — Peripeteia or Reversal of the Situation, and Recognition scenes — are parts of the plot. A further proof is, that novices in the art attain to finish of diction and precision of portraiture before they can construct the plot. It is the same with almost all the early poets.

The Plot, then, is the first principle, and, as it were,

the soul of a tragedy: Character holds the second place. A similar fact is seen in painting. The most beautiful colours, laid on confusedly, will not give as much pleasure as the chalk outline of a portrait. Thus Tragedy is the imitation of an action, and of the agents mainly with a view to the action.

Third in order is Thought, — that is, the faculty of saying what is possible and pertinent in given circumstances. In the case of oratory, this is the function of the political art and of the art of rhetoric: and so indeed the older poets make their characters speak the language of civic life; the poets of our time, the language of the rhetoricians. Character is that which reveals moral purpose, showing what kind of things a man chooses or avoids. Speeches, therefore, which do not make this manifest, or in which the speaker does not choose or avoid anything whatever, are not expressive of character. Thought, on the other hand, is found where something is proved to be or not to be, or a general maxim is enunciated.

Fourth among the elements enumerated comes Diction; by which I mean, as has been already said, the expression of the meaning in words; and its essence is the same both in verse and prose.

Of the remaining elements Song holds the chief place among the embellishments.

The Spectacle has, indeed, an emotional attraction of its own, but, of all the parts, it is the least artistic, and connected least with the art of poetry. For the power of Tragedy, we may be sure, is felt even apart from representation and actors. Besides, the production of spectacular effects depends more on the art of the stage machinist than on that of the poet.

VII

These principles being established, let us now discuss the proper structure of the Plot, since this is the first and most important thing in Tragedy.

Now, according to our definition, Tragedy is an imitation of an action that is complete, and whole, and of a certain magnitude; for there may be a whole that is wanting in magnitude. A whole is that which has a beginning, a middle, and an end. A beginning is that which does not itself follow anything by causal necessity, but after which something naturally is or comes to be. An end, on the contrary, is that which itself naturally follows some other thing, either by necessity, or as a rule, but has nothing following it. A middle is that which follows something as some other thing follows it. A well constructed plot, therefore, must neither begin nor end at haphazard, but conform to these principles.

Again, a beautiful object, whether it be a living organism or any whole composed of parts, must not only have an orderly arrangement of parts, but must also be of a certain magnitude; for beauty depends on magnitude and order. Hence a very small animal organism cannot be beautiful; for the view of it is confused, the object being seen in an almost imperceptible moment of time. Nor, again, can one of vast size be beautiful; for as the eye cannot take it all in at once, the unity and sense of the whole is lost for the spectator; as for instance if there were one a thousand miles long. As, therefore, in the case of animate bodies and organisms a certain magnitude is necessary, and a magnitude which may be easily embraced in one view; so in the plot, a certain length is necessary, and a length which can be easily embraced by the memory. The limit of length in relation to dramatic competition and sensuous presentment, is no part of artistic theory. For had it been the rule for a hundred tragedies to compete together, the performance would have been regulated by the water-clock, — as indeed we are told was formerly done. But the limit as fixed by the nature of the drama itself is this: — the greater the length, the more beautiful will the piece be by reason of its size, provided that the whole be perspicuous. And to define the matter roughly, we may say that the proper magnitude is comprised within such limits, that the sequence of events, according to the law of probability or necessity, will admit of a change from bad fortune to good, or from good fortune to bad.

VIII

Unity of plot does not, as some persons think, consist in the unity of the hero. For infinitely various are the incidents in one man's life which cannot be reduced to unity; and so, too, there are many actions of one man out of which we cannot make one action. Hence the error, as it appears, of all poets who have composed a Heracleid, a Theseid, or other poems of the kind. They imagine that as Heracles was one man, the story of Heracles must also be a unity. But Homer, as in all else he is of surpassing merit, here too — whether from art or natural genius — seems to have happily discerned the truth. In composing the Odyssey he did not include all the adventures of Odysseus — such as his wound on Parnassus, or his feigned madness at the mustering of the host — incidents between which there was no necessary or probable connexion: but he made the Odyssey, and likewise the Iliad, to centre round an action that in our sense of the word is one. As therefore, in the other imitative arts, the imitation is one when the object imitated is one, so the plot, being an imitation of an action, must imitate one action and that a whole, the structural union of the parts being such that, if any one of them is displaced or removed, the whole will be disjointed and disturbed. For a thing whose presence or absence makes no visible difference, is not an organic part of the whole.

IX

It is, moreover, evident from what has been said, that
it is not the function of the poet to relate what has
happened, but what may happen, — what is possible
according to the law of probability or necessity. The
poet and the historian differ not by writing in verse
or in prose. The work of Herodotus might be put into
verse, and it would still be a species of history, with
metre no less than without it. The true difference is
that one relates what has happened, the other what
may happen. Poetry, therefore, is a more philosophi-
cal and a higher thing than history: for poetry tends
to express the universal, history the particular. By the
universal I mean how a person of a certain type will
on occasion speak or act, according to the law of
probability or necessity; and it is this universality at
which poetry aims in the names she attaches to the
personages. The particular is — for example — what
Alcibiades did or suffered. In Comedy this is already
apparent: for here the poet first constructs the plot
on the lines of probability, and then inserts charac-
teristic names; — unlike the lampooners who write
about particular individuals. But tragedians still keep
to real names, the reason being that what is possible
is credible: what has not happened we do not at once
feel sure to be possible: but what has happened is
manifestly possible: otherwise it would not have hap-
pened. Still there are even some tragedies in which

there are only one or two well known names, the rest being fictitious. In others, none are well known, — as in Agathon's Antheus, where incidents and names alike are fictitious, and yet they give none the less pleasure. We must not, therefore, at all costs keep to the received legends, which are the usual subjects of Tragedy. Indeed, it would be absurd to attempt it; for even subjects that are known are known only to a few, and yet give pleasure to all. It clearly follows that the poet or 'maker' should be the maker of plots rather than of verses; since he is a poet because he imitates, and what he imitates are actions. And even if he chances to take an historical subject, he is none the less a poet; for there is no reason why some events that have actually happened should not conform to the law of the probable and possible, and in virtue of that quality in them he is their poet or maker.

Of all plots and actions the epeisodic are the worst. I call a plot 'epeisodic' in which the episodes or acts succeed one another without probable or necessary sequence. Bad poets compose such pieces by their own fault, good poets, to please the players; for, as they write show pieces for competition, they stretch the plot beyond its capacity, and are often forced to break the natural continuity.

But again, Tragedy is an imitation not only of a complete action, but of events inspiring fear or pity. Such an effect is best produced when the events come on us by surprise; and the effect is heightened when, at the same time, they follow as cause and effect. The tragic wonder will then be greater than if they happened of themselves or by accident; for even coincidences are most striking when they have an air of design. We may instance the statue of Mitys at Argos, which fell upon his murderer while he was a spectator at a festival, and killed him. Such events seem not to be due to mere chance. Plots, therefore, constructed on these principles are necessarily the best.

X

Plots are either Simple or Complex, for the actions in real life, of which the plots are an imitation, obviously show a similar distinction. An action which is one and continuous in the sense above defined, I call Simple, when the change of fortune takes place without Reversal of the Situation and without Recognition.

A Complex action is one in which the change is accompanied by such Reversal, or by Recognition, or by both. These last should arise from the internal structure of the plot, so that what follows should be the necessary or probable result of the preceding action. It makes all the difference whether any given event is a case of *propter hoc* or *post hoc*.

XI

Reversal of the Situation is a change by which the action veers round to its opposite, subject always to our rule of probability or necessity. Thus in the Oedipus, the messenger comes to cheer Oedipus and free him from his alarms about his mother, but by revealing who he is, he produces the opposite effect. Again in the Lynceus, Lynceus is being led away to his death, and Danaus goes with him, meaning to slay him; but the outcome of the preceding incidents is that Danaus is killed and Lynceus saved.

Recognition, as the name indicates, is a change from ignorance to knowledge, producing love or hate between the persons destined by the poet for good or bad fortune. The best form of recognition is coincident with a Reversal of the Situation, as in the Oedipus. There are indeed other forms. Even inanimate things of the most trivial kind may in a sense be objects of recognition. Again, we may recognise or discover whether a person has done a thing or not. But the recognition which is most intimately connected with the plot and action is, as we have said, the recognition of persons. This recognition, combined with Reversal, will produce either pity or fear; and actions producing these effects are those which, by our definition, Tragedy represents. Moreover, it is upon such situations that the issues of good or bad fortune will depend. Recognition, then, being between persons, it may happen that one person only is recognised by the other — when the latter is already known — or it may be necessary that the recognition should be on both sides. Thus Iphigenia is revealed to Orestes by the sending of the letter; but another act of recognition is required to make Orestes known to Iphigenia.

Two parts, then, of the Plot — Reversal of the Situation and Recognition — turn upon surprises. A third part is the Scene of Suffering. The Scene of Suffering is a destructive or painful action, such as death on the stage, bodily agony, wounds and the like.

XII

[The parts of Tragedy which must be treated as elements of the whole have been already mentioned. We now come to the quantitative parts — the separate parts into which Tragedy is divided — namely, Prologue, Episode, Exode, Choric song; this last being divided into Parode and Stasimon. These are common to all plays: peculiar to some are the songs of actors from the stage and the Commoi.

The Prologue is that entire part of a tragedy which precedes the Parode of the Chorus. The Episode is that entire part of a tragedy which is between complete choric songs. The Exode is that entire part of a tragedy which has no choric song after it. Of the Choric part the Parode is the first undivided utterance of the Chorus: the Stasimon is a Choric ode without anapaests or trochaic tetrameters: the Commos is a joint lamentation of Chorus and actors. The parts of Tragedy which must be treated as elements of the whole have been already mentioned. The quantitative parts — the separate parts into which it is divided — are here enumerated.]

XIII

As the sequel to what has already been said, we must proceed to consider what the poet should aim at, and what he should avoid, in constructing his plots; and by what means the specific effect of Tragedy will be produced.

A perfect tragedy should, as we have seen, be arranged not on the simple but on the complex plan. It should, moreover, imitate actions which excite pity and fear, this being the distinctive mark of tragic imitation. It follows plainly, in the first place, that the change of fortune presented must not be the spectacle of a virtuous man brought from prosperity to adversity: for this moves neither pity nor fear; it merely shocks us. Nor, again, that of a bad man passing from adversity to prosperity: for nothing can be more alien to the spirit of Tragedy; it possesses no single tragic quality; it neither satisfies the moral sense nor calls forth pity or fear. Nor, again, should the downfall of the utter villain be exhibited. A plot of this kind would, doubtless, satisfy the moral sense, but it would inspire neither pity nor fear; for pity is aroused by unmerited misfortune, fear by the misfortune of a man like ourselves. Such an event, therefore, will be neither pitiful nor terrible. There remains, then, the character between these two extremes, — that of a man who is not eminently good and just, yet whose misfortune is brought about not by vice or depravity, but by some error or frailty. He must be one who is highly renowned and prosperous, — a personage like Oedipus, Thyestes, or other illustrious men of such families.

A well constructed plot should, therefore, be single in its issue, rather than double as some maintain. The change of fortune should be not from bad to good, but, reversely, from good to bad. It should come about as the result not of vice, but of some great error or frailty, in a character either such as we have described, or better rather than worse. The practice of the stage bears out our view. At first the poets recounted any legend that came in their way. Now, the best tragedies are founded on the story of a few houses, — on the fortunes of Alcmaeon, Oedipus, Orestes, Meleager, Thyestes, Telephus, and those others who have done or suffered something terrible. A tragedy, then, to be perfect according to the rules of art should be of this construction. Hence they are in error who censure Euripides just because he follows this principle in his plays, many of which end unhappily. It is, as we have said, the right ending. The best proof is that on the stage and in dramatic competition, such plays, if well worked out, are the most tragic in effect; and Euripides, faulty though he may be in the general management of his subject, yet is felt to be the most tragic of the poets.

In the second rank comes the kind of tragedy which some place first. Like the Odyssey, it has a double thread of plot, and also an opposite catastrophe for the good and for the bad. It is accounted the best because of the weakness of the spectators; for the poet is guided in what he writes by the wishes of his audience. The pleasure, however, thence derived is not the true tragic pleasure. It is proper rather to Comedy, where those who, in the piece, are the deadliest enemies — like Orestes and Aegisthus — quit the stage as friends at the close, and no one slays or is slain.

XIV

Fear and pity may be aroused by spectacular means; but they may also result from the inner structure of the piece, which is the better way, and indicates a superior poet. For the plot ought to be so constructed

that, even without the aid of the eye, he who hears
the tale told will thrill with horror and melt to pity
at what takes place. This is the impression we should
receive from hearing the story of the Oedipus. But
to produce this effect by the mere spectacle is a less
artistic method, and dependent on extraneous aids.
Those who employ spectacular means to create a
sense not of the terrible but only of the monstrous,
are strangers to the purpose of Tragedy; for we must
not demand of Tragedy any and every kind of plea-
sure, but only that which is proper to it. And since the
pleasure which the poet should afford is that which
comes from pity and fear through imitation, it is evi-
dent that this quality must be impressed upon the
incidents.

Let us then determine what are the circumstances
which strike us as terrible or pitiful.

Actions capable of this effect must happen be-
tween persons who are either friends or enemies or
indifferent to one another. If an enemy kills an en-
emy, there is nothing to excite pity either in the act
or the intention, — except so far as the suffering in it-
self is pitiful. So again with indifferent persons. But
when the tragic incident occurs between those who
are near or dear to one another — if, for example, a
brother kills, or intends to kill, a brother, a son his fa-
ther, a mother her son, a son his mother, or any other
deed of the kind is done — these are the situations to
be looked for by the poet. He may not indeed destroy
the framework of the received legends — the fact, for

instance, that Clytemnestra was slain by Orestes and Eriphyle by Alcmaeon — but he ought to show invention of his own, and skilfully handle the traditional material. Let us explain more clearly what is meant by skilful handling.

The action may be done consciously and with knowledge of the persons, in the manner of the older poets. It is thus too that Euripides makes Medea slay her children. Or, again, the deed of horror may be done, but done in ignorance, and the tie of kinship or friendship be discovered afterwards. The Oedipus of Sophocles is an example. Here, indeed, the incident is outside the drama proper; but cases occur where it falls within the action of the play: one may cite the Alcmaeon of Astydamas, or Telegonus in the Wounded Odysseus. Again, there is a third case, — <to be about to act with knowledge of the persons and then not to act. The fourth case is>when some one is about to do an irreparable deed through ignorance, and makes the discovery before it is done. These are the only possible ways. For the deed must either be done or not done, — and that wittingly or unwittingly. But of all these ways, to be about to act knowing the persons, and then not to act, is the worst. It is shocking without being tragic, for no disaster follows. It is, therefore, never, or very rarely, found in poetry. One instance, however, is in the Antigone, where Haemon threatens to kill Creon. The next and better way is that the deed should be perpetrated. Still better, that it should be perpetrated in ignorance, and

the discovery made afterwards. There is then noth-
ing to shock us, while the discovery produces a star-
tling effect. The last case is the best, as when in the
Cresphontes Merope is about to slay her son, but, rec-
ognising who he is, spares his life. So in the Iphigenia,
the sister recognises the brother just in time. Again in
the Helle, the son recognises the mother when on the
point of giving her up. This, then, is why a few fami-
lies only, as has been already observed, furnish the
subjects of tragedy. It was not art, but happy chance,
that led the poets in search of subjects to impress the
tragic quality upon their plots. They are compelled,
therefore, to have recourse to those houses whose
history contains moving incidents like these.

Enough has now been said concerning the struc-
ture of the incidents, and the right kind of plot.

XV

In respect of Character there are four things to be
aimed at. First, and most important, it must be good.
Now any speech or action that manifests moral pur-
pose of any kind will be expressive of character: the
character will be good if the purpose is good. This
rule is relative to each class. Even a woman may be
good, and also a slave; though the woman may be
said to be an inferior being, and the slave quite worth-
less. The second thing to aim at is propriety. There

is a type of manly valour; but valour in a woman, or unscrupulous cleverness, is inappropriate. Thirdly, character must be true to life: for this is a distinct thing from goodness and propriety, as here described. The fourth point is consistency: for though the subject of the imitation, who suggested the type, be inconsistent, still he must be consistently inconsistent. As an example of motiveless degradation of character, we have Menelaus in the Orestes: of character indecorous and inappropriate, the lament of Odysseus in the Scylla, and the speech of Melanippe: of inconsistency, the Iphigenia at Aulis, — for Iphigenia the suppliant in no way resembles her later self.

As in the structure of the plot, so too in the portraiture of character, the poet should always aim either at the necessary or the probable. Thus a person of a given character should speak or act in a given way, by the rule either of necessity or of probability; just as this event should follow that by necessary or probable sequence. It is therefore evident that the unravelling of the plot, no less than the complication, must arise out of the plot itself, it must not be brought about by the *Deus ex Machina* — as in the Medea, or in the Return of the Greeks in the Iliad. The *Deus ex Machina* should be employed only for events external to the drama, — for antecedent or subsequent events, which lie beyond the range of human knowledge, and which require to be reported or foretold; for to the gods we ascribe the power of seeing all things. Within the action there must be nothing irrational. If the irrational cannot be excluded, it should be outside the scope of the tragedy. Such is the irrational element in the Oedipus of Sophocles.

Again, since Tragedy is an imitation of persons who are above the common level, the example of good portrait-painters should be followed. They, while reproducing the distinctive form of the original, make a likeness which is true to life and yet more beautiful. So too the poet, in representing men who are irascible or indolent, or have other defects of character, should preserve the type and yet ennoble it. In this way Achilles is portrayed by Agathon and Homer.

These then are rules the poet should observe. Nor should he neglect those appeals to the senses, which, though not among the essentials, are the concomitants of poetry; for here too there is much room for error. But of this enough has been said in our published treatises.

XVI

What Recognition is has been already explained. We will now enumerate its kinds.

First, the least artistic form, which, from poverty of wit, is most commonly employed — recognition

by signs. Of these some are congenital, — such as
'the spear which the earth-born race bear on their
bodies,' or the stars introduced by Carcinus in his
Thyestes. Others are acquired after birth; and of
these some are bodily marks, as scars; some exter-
nal tokens, as necklaces, or the little ark in the Tyro
by which the discovery is effected. Even these ad-
mit of more or less skilful treatment. Thus in the
recognition of Odysseus by his scar, the discovery is
made in one way by the nurse, in another by the
swineherds. The use of tokens for the express pur-
pose of proof — and, indeed, any formal proof with
or without tokens — is a less artistic mode of rec-
ognition. A better kind is that which comes about
by a turn of incident, as in the Bath Scene in the
Odyssey.

Next come the recognitions invented at will by the
poet, and on that account wanting in art. For exam-
ple, Orestes in the Iphigenia reveals the fact that he
is Orestes. She, indeed, makes herself known by the
letter; but he, by speaking himself, and saying what
the poet, not what the plot requires. This, therefore,
is nearly allied to the fault above mentioned: — for
Orestes might as well have brought tokens with him.
Another similar instance is the 'voice of the shuttle'
in the Tereus of Sophocles.

The third kind depends on memory when the sight
of some object awakens a feeling: as in the Cyprians
of Dicaeogenes, where the hero breaks into tears on
seeing the picture; or again in the 'Lay of Alcinous,'

where Odysseus, hearing the minstrel play the lyre, recalls the past and weeps; and hence the recognition.

The fourth kind is by process of reasoning. Thus in the Choëphori: — 'Some one resembling me has come: no one resembles me but Orestes: therefore Orestes has come.' Such too is the discovery made by Iphigenia in the play of Polyidus the Sophist. It was a natural reflexion for Orestes to make, 'So I too must die at the altar like my sister.' So, again, in the Tydeus of Theodectes, the father says, 'I came to find my son, and I lose my own life.' So too in the Phineidae: the women, on seeing the place, inferred their fate: — 'Here we are doomed to die, for here we were cast forth.' Again, there is a composite kind of recognition involving false inference on the part of one of the characters, as in the Odysseus Disguised as a Messenger. A said <that no one else was able to bend the bow; ... hence B (the disguised Odysseus) imagined that A would> recognise the bow which, in fact, he had not seen; and to bring about a recognition by this means — the expectation that A would recognise the bow — is false inference.

But, of all recognitions, the best is that which arises from the incidents themselves, where the startling discovery is made by natural means. Such is that in the Oedipus of Sophocles, and in the Iphigenia; for it was natural that Iphigenia should wish to dispatch a letter. These recognitions alone dispense with the

artificial aid of tokens or amulets. Next come the
recognitions by process of reasoning.

XVII

In constructing the plot and working it out with the
proper diction, the poet should place the scene, as far
as possible, before his eyes. In this way, seeing every-
thing with the utmost vividness, as if he were a spec-
tator of the action, he will discover what is in keeping
with it, and be most unlikely to overlook inconsis-
tencies. The need of such a rule is shown by the fault
found in Carcinus. Amphiaraus was on his way from
the temple. This fact escaped the observation of one
who did not see the situation. On the stage, however,
the piece failed, the audience being offended at the
oversight.

Again, the poet should work out his play, to the best
of his power, with appropriate gestures; for those who
feel emotion are most convincing through natural
sympathy with the characters they represent; and one
who is agitated storms, one who is angry rages, with
the most life-like reality. Hence poetry implies either
a happy gift of nature or a strain of madness. In the
one case a man can take the mould of any character;
in the other, he is lifted out of his proper self.

As for the story, whether the poet takes it ready

made or constructs it for himself, he should first sketch its general outline, and then fill in the episodes and amplify in detail. The general plan may be illustrated by the Iphigenia. A young girl is sacrificed; she disappears mysteriously from the eyes of those who sacrificed her; she is transported to another country, where the custom is to offer up all strangers to the goddess. To this ministry she is appointed. Some time later her own brother chances to arrive. The fact that the oracle for some reason ordered him to go there, is outside the general plan of the play. The purpose, again, of his coming is outside the action proper. However, he comes, he is seized, and, when on the point of being sacrificed, reveals who he is. The mode of recognition may be either that of Euripides or of Polyidus, in whose play he exclaims very naturally: — 'So it was not my sister only, but I too, who was doomed to be sacrificed'; and by that remark he is saved.

After this, the names being once given, it remains to fill in the episodes. We must see that they are relevant to the action. In the case of Orestes, for example, there is the madness which led to his capture, and his deliverance by means of the purificatory rite. In the drama, the episodes are short, but it is these that give extension to Epic poetry. Thus the story of the Odyssey can be stated briefly. A certain man is absent from home for many years; he is jealously watched by Poseidon, and left desolate. Meanwhile his home is in a wretched plight — suitors are wasting his substance and plotting against his son. At length, tempest-tost, he himself arrives; he makes certain persons acquainted with him; he attacks the suitors with his own hand, and is himself preserved while he destroys them. This is the essence of the plot; the rest is episode.

XVIII

Every tragedy falls into two parts, — Complication and Unravelling or *Dénouement*. Incidents ·extraneous to the action are frequently combined with a portion of the action proper, to form the Complication; the rest is the Unravelling. By the Complication I mean all that extends from the beginning of the action to the part which marks the turning-point to good or bad fortune. The Unravelling is that which extends from the beginning of the change to the end. Thus, in the Lynceus of Theodectes, the Complication consists of the incidents presupposed in the drama, the seizure of the child, and then again * * <The Unravelling> extends from the accusation of murder to the end.

There are four kinds of Tragedy, the Complex, depending entirely on Reversal of the Situation and Recognition; the Pathetic (where the motive is passion), — such as the tragedies on Ajax and Ixion;

the Ethical (where the motives are ethical), — such as the Phthiotides and the Peleus. The fourth kind is the Simple. <We here exclude the purely spectacular element>, exemplified by the Phorcides, the Prometheus, and scenes laid in Hades. The poet should endeavour, if possible, to combine all poetic elements; or failing that, the greatest number and those the most important; the more so, in face of the cavilling criticism of the day. For whereas there have hitherto been good poets, each in his own branch, the critics now expect one man to surpass all others in their several lines of excellence.

In speaking of a tragedy as the same or different, the best test to take is the plot. Identity exists where the Complication and Unravelling are the same. Many poets tie the knot well, but unravel it ill. Both arts, however, should always be mastered.

Again, the poet should remember what has been often said, and not make an Epic structure into a Tragedy — by an Epic structure I mean one with a multiplicity of plots — as if, for instance, you were to make a tragedy out of the entire story of the Iliad. In the Epic poem, owing to its length, each part assumes its proper magnitude. In the drama the result is far from answering to the poet's expectation. The proof is that the poets who have dramatised the whole story of the Fall of Troy, instead of selecting portions, like Euripides; or who have taken the whole tale of Niobe, and not a part of her story, like Aeschylus, either fail utterly or meet with poor success on the

stage. Even Agathon has been known to fail from
this one defect. In his Reversals of the Situation,
however, he shows a marvellous skill in the effort
to hit the popular taste, — to produce a tragic effect
that satisfies the moral sense. This effect is produced
when the clever rogue, like Sisyphus, is outwitted,
or the brave villain defeated. Such an event is prob-
able in Agathon's sense of the word: 'it is probable,'
he says, 'that many things should happen contrary to
probability.'

The Chorus too should be regarded as one of the
actors; it should be an integral part of the whole, and
share in the action, in the manner not of Euripides
but of Sophocles. As for the later poets, their choral
songs pertain as little to the subject of the piece as to
that of any other tragedy. They are, therefore, sung as
mere interludes, — a practice first begun by Agathon.
Yet what difference is there between introducing
such choral interludes, and transferring a speech, or
even a whole act, from one play to another?

XIX

It remains to speak of Diction and Thought, the other
parts of Tragedy having been already discussed. Con-
cerning Thought, we may assume what is said in the
Rhetoric, to which inquiry the subject more strictly

belongs. Under Thought is included every effect which has to be produced by speech, the subdivisions being, — proof and refutation; the excitation of the feelings, such as pity, fear, anger, and the like; the suggestion of importance or its opposite. Now, it is evident that the dramatic incidents must be treated from the same points of view as the dramatic speeches, when the object is to evoke the sense of pity, fear, importance, or probability. The only difference is, that the incidents should speak for themselves without verbal exposition; while the effects aimed at in speech should be produced by the speaker, and as a result of the speech. For what were the business of a speaker, if the Thought were revealed quite apart from what he says?

Next, as regards Diction. One branch of the inquiry treats of the Modes of Utterance. But this province of knowledge belongs to the art of Delivery and to the masters of that science. It includes, for instance, — what is a command, a prayer, a statement, a threat, a question, an answer, and so forth. To know or not to know these things involves no serious censure upon the poet's art. For who can admit the fault imputed to Homer by Protagoras, — that in the words, 'Sing, goddess, of the wrath,' he gives a command under the idea that he utters a prayer? For to tell some one to do a thing or not to do it is, he says, a command. We may, therefore, pass this over as an inquiry that belongs to another art, not to poetry.

XX

[Language in general includes the following parts: — Letter, Syllable, Connecting word, Noun, Verb, Inflexion or Case, Sentence or Phrase.

A Letter is an indivisible sound, yet not every such sound, but only one which can form part of a group of sounds. For even brutes utter indivisible sounds, none of which I call a letter. The sound I mean may be either a vowel, a semi-vowel, or a mute. A vowel is that which without impact of tongue or lip has an audible sound. A semi-vowel, that which with such impact has an audible sound, as S and R. A mute, that which with such impact has by itself no sound, but joined to a vowel sound becomes audible, as G and D. These are distinguished according to the form assumed by the mouth and the place where they are produced; according as they are aspirated or smooth, long or short; as they are acute, grave, or of an intermediate tone; which inquiry belongs in detail to the writers on metre.

A Syllable is a non-significant sound, composed of a mute and a vowel: for GR without A is a syllable, as also with A, — GRA. But the investigation of these differences belongs also to metrical science.

A Connecting word is a non-significant sound, which neither causes nor hinders the union of many sounds into one significant sound; it may be placed at either end or in the middle of a sentence. Or, a non-significant sound, which out of several sounds, each of them significant, is capable of forming one significant sound, — as ἀμφί, περί,[1] and the like. Or, a non-significant sound, which marks the beginning, end, or division of a sentence; such, however, that it cannot correctly stand by itself at the beginning of a sentence, — as μέν, ἤτοι, δέ.[2]

A Noun is a composite significant sound, not marking time, of which no part is in itself significant: for in double or compound words we do not employ the separate parts as if each were in itself significant. Thus in Theodorus, 'god-given,' the δῶρον or 'gift' is not in itself significant.

A Verb is a composite significant sound, marking time, in which, as in the noun, no part is in itself significant. For 'man,' or 'white' does not express the idea of 'when'; but 'he walks,' or 'he has walked' does connote time, present or past.

Inflexion belongs both to the noun and verb, and expresses either the relation 'of,' 'to,' or the like; or that of number, whether one or many, as 'man' or 'men'; or the modes or tones in actual delivery, e.g. a question or a command. 'Did he go?' and 'go' are verbal inflexions of this kind.

A Sentence or Phrase is a composite significant sound, some at least of whose parts are in themselves

---

[1] "Around," "about."
[2] Untranslatable "particles" adding flavor or clarifying sentence structure.

significant; for not every such group of words consists
of verbs and nouns — 'the definition of man,' for ex-
ample — but it may dispense even with the verb. Still
it will always have some significant part, as 'in walk-
ing,' or 'Cleon son of Cleon.' A sentence or phrase
may form a unity in two ways, — either as signifying
one thing, or as consisting of several parts linked to-
gether. Thus the Iliad is one by the linking together of
parts, the definition of man by the unity of the thing
signified.]

XXI

Words are of two kinds, simple and double. By sim-
ple I mean those composed of non-significant ele-
ments, such as $\gamma \tilde{\eta}$.[3] By double or compound, those
composed either of a significant and non-significant
element (though within the whole word no element
is significant), or of elements that are both signifi-
cant. A word may likewise be triple, quadruple, or
multiple in form, like so many Massilian expressions,
e.g. 'Hermo-caico-xanthus <who prayed to Father
Zeus>.'

Every word is either current, or strange, or meta-
phorical, or ornamental, or newly-coined, or
lengthened, or contracted, or altered.

---

[3] "Earth."

By a current or proper word I mean one which is in'
general use among a people; by a strange word, one
which is in use in another country. Plainly, therefore,
the same word may be at once strange and current,
but not in relation to the same people. The word
σίγυνον, 'lance,' is to the Cyprians a current term
but to us a strange one.

Metaphor is the application of an alien name by
transference either from genus to species, or from spe-
cies to genus, or from species to species, or by analogy,
that is, proportion. Thus from genus to species, as:
'There lies my ship'; for lying at anchor is a species of
lying. From species to genus, as: 'Verily ten thousand
noble deeds hath Odysseus wrought'; for ten thou-
sand is a species of large number, and is here used for
a large number generally. From species to species, as:
'With blade of bronze drew away the life,' and 'Cleft
the water with the vessel of unyielding bronze.' Here
ἀρύσαι, 'to draw away,' is used for ταμεῖν, 'to cleave,'
and ταμεῖν again for ἀρύσαι, — each being a species
of taking away. Analogy or proportion is when the
second term is to the first as the fourth to the third.
We may then use the fourth for the second, or the
second for the fourth. Sometimes too we qualify the
metaphor by adding the term to which the proper
word is relative. Thus the cup is to Dionysus as the
shield to Ares. The cup may, therefore, be called
'the shield of Dionysus,' and the shield 'the cup of
Ares.' Or, again, as old age is to life, so is evening to
day. Evening may therefore be called 'the old age of

the day,' and old age, 'the evening of life,' or, in the phrase of Empedocles, 'life's setting sun.' For some of the terms of the proportion there is at times no word in existence; still the metaphor may be used. For instance, to scatter seed is called sowing: but the action of the sun in scattering his rays is nameless. Still this process bears to the sun the same relation as sowing to the seed. Hence the expression of the poet 'sowing the god-created light.' There is another way in which this kind of metaphor may be employed. We may apply an alien term, and then deny of that term one of its proper attributes; as if we were to call the shield, not 'the cup of Ares,' but 'the wineless cup.'

<An ornamental word . . .>

A newly-coined word is one which has never been even in local use, but is adopted by the poet himself. Some such words there appear to be: as ἐρνύγες, 'sprouters,' for κέρατα, 'horns,' and ἀρητήρ, 'supplicator,' for ἱερεύς, 'priest.'

A word is lengthened when its own vowel is exchanged for a longer one, or when a syllable is inserted. A word is contracted when some part of it is removed. Instances of lengthening are, — πόληος for πόλεως,[4] and Πηληιάδεω for Πηλείδου:[5] of contraction, — κρῖ, δῶ, and ὄψ,[6] as in μία γίνεται ἀμφοτέρων ὄψ.[7]

---

[4] "Of the city."
[5] "Of the son of Peleus [i.e., Achilles]."
[6] "Barley," "house," "face."
[7] "The appearance of both of them becomes a single one."

An altered word is one in which part of the ordinary form is left unchanged, and part is re-cast; as in δεξιτερὸν κατὰ μαζόν,[8] δεξιτερόν is for δεξιόν.[9]

[Nouns in themselves are either masculine, feminine, or neuter. Masculine are such as end in ν, ρ, ς, or in some letter compounded with ς, — these being two, ψ and ξ. Feminine, such as end in vowels that are always long, namely η and ω, and — of vowels that admit of lengthening — those in α. Thus the number of letters in which nouns masculine and feminine end is the same; for ψ and ξ are equivalent to endings in ς. No noun ends in a mute or a vowel short by nature. Three only end in ι, — μέλι, κόμμι, πέπερι:[10] five end in υ. Neuter nouns end in these two latter vowels; also in ν and ς.]

XXII

The perfection of style is to be clear without being mean. The clearest style is that which uses only current or proper words; at the same time it is mean: — witness the poetry of Cleophon and of Sthenelus. That diction, on the other hand, is lofty

---

[8] "On the right-hand breast."
[9] "Right."
[10] "Honey," "gum," "pepper."

and raised above the commonplace which employs unusual words. By unusual, I mean strange (or rare) words, metaphorical, lengthened, — anything, in short, that differs from the normal idiom. Yet a style wholly composed of such words is either a riddle or a jargon; a riddle, if it consists of metaphors; a jargon, if it consists of strange (or rare) words. For the essence of a riddle is to express true facts under impossible combinations. Now this cannot be done by any arrangement of ordinary words, but by the use of metaphor it can. Such is the riddle: — 'A man I saw who on another man had glued the bronze by aid of fire,' and others of the same kind. A diction that is made up of strange (or rare) terms is a jargon. A certain infusion, therefore, of these elements is necessary to style; for the strange (or rare) word, the metaphorical, the ornamental, and the other kinds above mentioned, will raise it above the commonplace and mean, while the use of proper words will make it perspicuous. But nothing contributes more to produce a clearness of diction that is remote from commonness than the lengthening, contraction, and alteration of words. For by deviating in exceptional cases from the normal idiom, the language will gain distinction; while, at the same time, the partial conformity with usage will give perspicuity. The critics, therefore, are in error who censure these licenses of speech, and hold the author up to ridicule. Thus Eucleides, the elder, declared that it would be an easy matter to be a poet if you might lengthen syllables at will. He caricatured the practice in the very form of his diction, as in the verse:

Ἐπιχάρην εἶδον Μαραθῶνάδε βαδίζοντα,[11]

or,

οὐκ ἄν γ᾽ ἐράμενος τὸν ἐκείνου ἐλλέβορον.[12]

To employ such license at all obtrusively is, no doubt, grotesque; but in any mode of poetic diction there must be moderation. Even metaphors, strange (or rare) words, or any similar forms of speech, would produce the like effect if used without propriety and with the express purpose of being ludicrous. How great a difference is made by the appropriate use of lengthening, may be seen in Epic poetry by the insertion of ordinary forms in the verse. So, again, if we take a strange (or rare) word, a metaphor, or any similar mode of expression, and replace it by the current or proper term, the truth of our observation will be manifest. For example Aeschylus and Euripides each composed the same iambic line. But the alteration of a single word by Euripides, who employed the rarer term instead of the ordinary one, makes one verse appear beautiful and the other trivial. Aeschylus in his Philoctetes says:

φαγέδαινα <δ᾽> ἥ μου σάρκας ἐσθίει ποδός.[13]

Euripides substitutes θοινᾶται 'feasts on' for ἐσθίει 'feeds on.' Again, in the line,

---

[11] "I saw Epichares walking toward Marathon."
[12] "But not if lusting after that man's hellebore."
[13] "The canker that consumes the flesh of my foot."

νῦν δέ μ' ἐὼν ὀλίγος τε καὶ οὐτιδανὸς καὶ
                    ἀεικής,[14]

the difference will be felt if we substitute the common words,

νῦν δέ μ' ἐὼν μικρός τε καὶ ἀσθενικὸς καὶ
                    'αειδής.[15]

Or, if for the line,

δίφρον ἀεικέλιον καταθεὶς ὀλίγην τε
                    τράπεζαν,[16]

we read,

δίφρον μοχθηρὸν καταθεὶς μικράν τε
                    τράπεζαν.[17]

Or, for ἠιόνες βοόωσιν, ἠιόνες κράζουσιν.[18]

Again, Ariphrades ridiculed the tragedians for using phrases which no one would employ in ordinary speech: for example, δωμάτων ἄπο[19] instead of ἀπὸ δωμάτων, σέθεν,[20] 'εγὼ δέ νιν,[21] Ἀχιλλέως πέρι[22] instead of περὶ Ἀχιλλέως, and the like. It is precisely because such phrases are not part of the current idiom that they give distinction to the style. This, however, he failed to see.

It is a great matter to observe propriety in these several modes of expression, as also in compound words,

---

14 "Now, being little, of no account and unseemly."
15 "Now, being small, weakly and unsightly."
16 "Having placed an unseemly seat and a scanty table."
17 "Having placed an inferior seat and an inadequate table."
18 "The shores roar," "the shores cry out."
19 "Away from the house."
20 "Your."
21 "I [answered] him (or her)."
22 "Concerning Achilles."

strange (or rare) words, and so forth. But the greatest thing by far is to have a command of metaphor. This alone cannot be imparted by another; it is the mark of genius, for to make good metaphors implies an eye for resemblances.

Of the various kinds of words, the compound are best adapted to dithyrambs, rare words to heroic poetry, metaphors to iambic. In heroic poetry, indeed, all these varieties are serviceable. But in iambic verse, which reproduces, as far as may be, familiar speech, the most appropriate words are those which are found even in prose. These are, — the current or proper, the metaphorical, the ornamental.

Concerning Tragedy and imitation by means of action this may suffice.

XXIII

As to that poetic imitation which is narrative in form and employs a single metre, the plot manifestly ought, as in a tragedy, to be constructed on dramatic principles. It should have for its subject a single action, whole and complete, with a beginning, a middle, and an end. It will thus resemble a living organism in all its unity, and produce the pleasure proper to it. It will differ in structure from historical compositions, which of necessity present not a single action, but a single period, and all that happened within that period to one person or to many, little connected together as the events may be. For as the sea-fight at Salamis and the battle with the Carthaginians in Sicily took place at the same time, but did not tend to any one result, so in the sequence of events, one thing sometimes follows another, and yet no single result is thereby produced. Such is the practice, we may say, of most poets. Here again, then, as has been already observed, the transcendent excellence of Homer is manifest. He never attempts to make the whole war of Troy the subject of his poem, though that war had a beginning and an end. It would have been too vast a theme, and not easily embraced in a single view. If, again, he had kept it within moderate limits, it must have been over-complicated by the variety of the incidents. As it is, he detaches a single portion, and admits as episodes many events from the general story of the war — such as the Catalogue of the ships and others — thus diversifying the poem. All other poets take a single hero, a single period, or an action single indeed, but with a multiplicity of parts. Thus did the author of the Cypria and of the Little Iliad. For this reason the Iliad and the Odyssey each furnish the subject of one tragedy, or, at most, of two; while the Cypria supplies materials for many, and the Little Iliad for eight — the Award of the Arms, the Philoctetes, the Neoptolemus, the Eurypylus, the Mendicant Odysseus, the Laconian Women, the Fall of Ilium, the Departure of the Fleet.

XXIV

Again, Epic poetry must have as many kinds as Tragedy: it must be simple, or complex, or 'ethical,' or 'pathetic.' The parts also, with the exception of song and spectacle, are the same; for it requires Reversals of the Situation, Recognitions, and Scenes of Suffering. Moreover, the thoughts and the diction must be artistic. In all these respects Homer is our earliest and sufficient model. Indeed each of his poems has a twofold character. The Iliad is at once simple and 'pathetic,' and the Odyssey complex (for Recognition scenes run through it), and at the same time 'ethical.' Moreover, in diction and thought they are supreme.

Epic poetry differs from Tragedy in the scale on which it is constructed, and in its metre. As regards scale or length, we have already laid down an adequate limit: — the beginning and the end must be capable of being brought within a single view. This condition will be satisfied by poems on a smaller scale than the old epics, and answering in length to the group of tragedies presented at a single sitting.

Epic poetry has, however, a great — a special — capacity for enlarging its dimensions, and we can see the reason. In Tragedy we cannot imitate several lines of actions carried on at one and the same time; we must confine ourselves to the action on the stage

and the part taken by the players. But in Epic po-
etry, owing to the narrative form, many events sim-
ultaneously transacted can be presented; and these,
if relevant to the subject, add mass and dignity to
the poem. The Epic has here an advantage, and one
that conduces to grandeur of effect, to diverting the
mind of the hearer, and relieving the story with vary-
ing episodes. For sameness of incident soon produces
satiety, and makes tragedies fail on the stage.

As for the metre, the heroic measure has proved its
fitness by the test of experience. If a narrative poem
in any other metre or in many metres were now
composed, it would be found incongruous. For of
all measures the heroic is the stateliest and the most
massive; and hence it most readily admits rare words
and metaphors, which is another point in which the
narrative form of imitation stands alone. On the other
hand, the iambic and the trochaic tetrameter are stir-
ring measures, the latter being akin to dancing, the
former expressive of action. Still more absurd would
it be to mix together different metres, as was done
by Chaeremon. Hence no one has ever composed a
poem on a great scale in any other than heroic verse.
Nature herself, as we have said, teaches the choice of
the proper measure.

Homer, admirable in all respects, has the special
merit of being the only poet who rightly appreciates
the part he should take himself. The poet should
speak as little as possible in his own person, for it
is not this that makes him an imitator. Other poets

appear themselves upon the scene throughout, and imitate but little and rarely. Homer, after a few prefatory words, at once brings in a man, or woman, or other personage; none of them wanting in characteristic qualities, but each with a character of his own.

The element of the wonderful is required in Tragedy. The irrational, on which the wonderful depends for its chief effects, has wider scope in Epic poetry, because there the person acting is not seen. Thus, the pursuit of Hector would be ludicrous if placed upon the stage — the Greeks standing still and not joining in the pursuit, and Achilles waving them back. But in the Epic poem the absurdity passes unnoticed. Now the wonderful is pleasing: as may be inferred from the fact that every one tells a story with some addition of his own, knowing that his hearers like it. It is Homer who has chiefly taught other poets the art of telling lies skilfully. The secret of it lies in a fallacy. For, assuming that if one thing is or becomes, a second is or becomes, men imagine that, if the second is, the first likewise is or becomes. But this is a false inference. Hence, where the first thing is untrue, it is quite unnecessary, provided the second be true, to add that the first is or has become. For the mind, knowing the second to be true, falsely infers the truth of the first. There is an example of this in the Bath Scene of the Odyssey.

Accordingly, the poet should prefer probable impossibilities to improbable possibilities. The tragic plot must not be composed of irrational parts. Everything irrational should, if possible, be excluded; or, at all events, it should lie outside the action of the play (as, in the Oedipus, the hero's ignorance as to the manner of Laius' death); not within the drama, — as in the Electra, the messenger's account of the Pythian games; or, as in the Mysians, the man who has come from Tegea to Mysia and is still speechless. The plea that otherwise the plot would have been ruined, is ridiculous; such a plot should not in the first instance be constructed. But once the irrational has been introduced and an air of likelihood imparted to it, we must accept it in spite of the absurdity. Take even the irrational incidents in the Odyssey, where Odysseus is left upon the shore of Ithaca. How intolerable even these might have been would be apparent if an inferior poet were to treat the subject. As it is, the absurdity is veiled by the poetic charm with which the poet invests it.

The diction should be elaborated in the pauses of the action, where there is no expression of character or thought. For, conversely, character and thought are merely obscured by a diction that is over brilliant.

XXV

With respect to critical difficulties and their solutions, the number and nature of the sources from which they may be drawn may be thus exhibited.

The poet being an imitator, like a painter or any other artist, must of necessity imitate one of three objects, — things as they were or are, things as they are said or thought to be, or things as they ought to be. The vehicle of expression is language, — either current terms or, it may be, rare words or metaphors. There are also many modifications of language, which we concede to the poets. Add to this, that the standard of correctness is not the same in poetry and politics, any more than in poetry and any other art. Within the art of poetry itself there are two kinds of faults, — those which touch its essence, and those which are accidental. If a poet has chosen to imitate something, <but has imitated it incorrectly> through want of capacity, the error is inherent in the poetry. But if the failure is due to a wrong choice — if he has represented a horse as throwing out both his off legs at once, or introduced technical inaccuracies in medicine, for example, or in any other art — the error is not essential to the poetry. These are the points of view from which we should consider and answer the objections raised by the critics.

First as to matters which concern the poet's own art. If he describes the impossible, he is guilty of an error; but the error may be justified, if the end of the art be thereby attained (the end being that already mentioned), — if, that is, the effect of this or any other part of the poem is thus rendered more striking. A case in point is the pursuit of Hector. If, however, the end might have been as well, or better, attained without violating the special rules of the poetic art, the error is not justified: for every kind of error should, if possible, be avoided.

Again, does the error touch the essentials of the poetic art, or some accident of it? For example, — not to know that a hind has no horns is a less serious matter than to paint it inartistically.

Further, if it be objected that the description is not true to fact, the poet may perhaps reply, — 'But the objects are as they ought to be': just as Sophocles said that he drew men as they ought to be; Euripides, as they are. In this way the objection may be met. If, however, the representation be of neither kind, the poet may answer, — 'This is how men say the thing is.' This applies to tales about the gods. It may well be that these stories are not higher than fact nor yet true to fact: they are, very possibly, what Xenophanes says of them. But anyhow, 'this is what is said.' Again, a description may be no better than the fact: still, it was the fact; as in the passage about the arms: 'Upright upon their butt-ends stood the spears.' This was the custom then, as it now is among the Illyrians.

Again, in examining whether what has been said or done by some one is poetically right or not, we must not look merely to the particular act or saying, and ask whether it is poetically good or bad. We must also consider by whom it is said or done, to whom, when, by what means, or for what end; whether, for instance, it be to secure a greater good, or avert a greater evil.

Other difficulties may be resolved by due regard to the usage of language. We may note a rare word, as in οὐρῆας μὲν πρῶτον,[23] where the poet perhaps employs οὐρῆας not in the sense of mules, but of sentinels. So, again, of Dolon: 'ill-favoured indeed he was to look upon.' It is not meant that his body was ill-shaped, but that his face was ugly; for the Cretans use the word εὐειδές, 'well-favoured,' to denote a fair face. Again, ζωρότερον δὲ κέραιε, 'mix the drink livelier,' does not mean 'mix it stronger' as for hard drinkers, but 'mix it quicker.'

Sometimes an expression is metaphorical, as 'Now all gods and men were sleeping through the night,' — while at the same time the poet says: 'Often indeed as he turned his gaze to the Trojan plain, he marvelled at the sound of flutes and pipes.' 'All' is here used metaphorically for 'many,' all being a species of many. So in the verse, — 'alone she hath no part . . .,' οἴη, 'alone,' is metaphorical; for the best known may be called the only one.

Again, the solution may depend upon accent or

---

[23] The first word is explained in the text; the rest of the phrase means "first."

breathing. Thus Hippias of Thasos solved the diffi-
culties in the lines, — δίδομεν (διδόμεν) δέ οἱ,[24] and
τὸ μὲν οὗ (οὐ) καταπύθεται ὄμβρῳ.[25]

Or again, the question may be solved by punctu-
ation, as in Empedocles, — 'Of a sudden things be-
came mortal that before had learnt to be immortal,
and things unmixed before mixed.'

Or again, by ambiguity of meaning, — as
παρῴχηκεν δὲ πλέω νύξ,[26] where the word πλέω
is ambiguous.

Or by the usage of language. Thus any mixed drink
is called οἶνος, 'wine.' Hence Ganymede is said 'to
pour the wine to Zeus,' though the gods do not drink
wine. So too workers in iron are called χαλκέας, or
workers in bronze. This, however, may also be taken
as a metaphor.

Again, when a word seems to involve some incon-
sistency of meaning, we should consider how many
senses it may bear in the particular passage. For ex-
ample: 'there was stayed the spear of bronze' — we
should ask in how many ways we may take 'being
checked there.' The true mode of interpretation is the
precise opposite of what Glaucon mentions. Critics,
he says, jump at certain groundless conclusions; they
pass adverse judgment and then proceed to reason
on it; and, assuming that the poet has said whatever

---

[24] "We give to him"/"Give to him!"
[25] "[The wood] of which is rotted by rain"/"Which is not rotted by rain."
[26] "Much/More of the night has gone by."

they happen to think, find fault if a thing is inconsistent with their own fancy. The question about Icarius has been treated in this fashion. The critics imagine he was a Lacedaemonian. They think it strange, therefore, that Telemachus should not have met him when he went to Lacedaemon. But the Cephallenian story may perhaps be the true one. They allege that Odysseus took a wife from among themselves, and that her father was Icadius not Icarius. It is merely a mistake, then, that gives plausibility to the objection.

In general, the impossible must be justified by reference to artistic requirements, or to the higher reality, or to received opinion. With respect to the requirements of art, a probable impossibility is to be preferred to a thing improbable and yet possible. Again, it may be impossible that there should be men such as Zeuxis painted. 'Yes,' we say, 'but the impossible is the higher thing; for the ideal type must surpass the reality.' To justify the irrational, we appeal to what is commonly said to be. In addition to which, we urge that the irrational sometimes does not violate reason; just as 'it is probable that a thing may happen contrary to probability.'

Things that sound contradictory should be examined by the same rules as in dialectical refutation — whether the same thing is meant, in the same relation, and in the same sense. We should therefore solve the question by reference to what the poet says himself, or to what is tacitly assumed by a person of intelligence.

The element of the irrational, and, similarly, depravity of character, are justly censured when there is no inner necessity for introducing them. Such is the irrational element in the introduction of Aegeus by Euripides and the badness of Menelaus in the Orestes.

Thus, there are five sources from which critical objections are drawn. Things are censured either as impossible, or irrational, or morally hurtful, or contradictory, or contrary to artistic correctness. The answers should be sought under the twelve heads above mentioned.

XXVI

The question may be raised whether the Epic or Tragic mode of imitation is the higher. If the more refined art is the higher, and the more refined in every case is that which appeals to the better sort of audience, the art which imitates anything and everything is manifestly most unrefined. The audience is supposed to be too dull to comprehend unless something of their own is thrown in by the performers, who therefore indulge in restless movements. Bad flute-players twist and twirl, if they have to represent 'the quoit-throw,' or hustle the coryphaeus when they perform the 'Scylla.' Tragedy, it is said, has this same defect. We may compare the opinion that the older actors entertained of their successors. Mynniscus used to call Callippides 'ape' on account of the extravagance of his action, and the same view was held of Pindarus. Tragic art, then, as a whole, stands to Epic in the same relation as the younger to the elder actors. So we are told that Epic poetry is addressed to a cultivated audience, who do not need gesture; Tragedy, to an inferior public. Being then unrefined, it is evidently the lower of the two.

Now, in the first place, this censure attaches not to the poetic but to the histrionic art; for gesticulation may be equally overdone in epic recitation, as by Sosistratus, or in lyrical competition, as by Mnasitheus the Opuntian. Next, all action is not to be condemned — any more than all dancing — but only that of bad performers. Such was the fault found in Callippides, as also in others of our own day, who are censured for representing degraded women. Again, Tragedy like Epic poetry produces its effect even without action; it reveals its power by mere reading. If, then, in all other respects it is superior, this fault, we say, is not inherent in it.

And superior it is, because it has all the epic elements — it may even use the epic metre — with the music and spectacular effects as important accessories; and these produce the most vivid of pleasures. Further, it has vividness of impression in reading as well as in representation. Moreover, the art attains its end within narrower limits; for the concentrated effect is more pleasurable than one which is spread over a long time and so diluted. What, for example, would be the effect of the Oedipus of Sophocles, if it were cast into a form as long as the Iliad? Once more, the Epic imitation has less unity; as is shown by this, that any Epic poem will furnish subjects for several tragedies. Thus if the story adopted by the poet has a strict unity, it must either be concisely told and appear truncated; or, if it conform to the Epic canon of length, it must seem weak and watery. <Such length implies some loss of unity,> if, I mean, the poem is constructed out of several actions, like the Iliad and the Odyssey, which have many such parts, each with a certain magnitude of its own. Yet these poems are as perfect as possible in structure; each is, in the highest degree attainable, an imitation of a single action.

If, then, Tragedy is superior to Epic poetry in all these respects, and, moreover, fulfils its specific function better as an art — for each art ought to produce, not any chance pleasure, but the pleasure proper to it, as already stated — it plainly follows that Tragedy is the higher art, as attaining its end more perfectly.

Thus much may suffice concerning Tragic and Epic poetry in general; their several kinds and parts, with the number of each and their differences; the causes that make a poem good or bad; the objections of the critics and the answers to these objections. * * *